Written by Peter Batson and Brian Batson
Designed by Bill Henderson, Deena Fleming, and Flora Chan

an imprint of
■SCHOLASTIC
www.scholastic.com

Scholastic and Tangerine Press and associated logos are trademarks of Scholastic Inc.

Published by Tangerine Press, an imprint of Scholastic Inc., 557 Broadway; New York, NY 10012

10 9 8 7 6 5 4 3 2 1

ISBN-10: 0-545-08504-7
ISBN-13: 978-0-545-08504-5

Printed and bound in China

Scholastic Canada, Ltd.
Markham, Ontario

Scholastic Australia Pty. Ltd
Gosford NSW

Scholastic New Zealand, Ltd.
Greenmount, Auckland

About the Authors

Peter Batson is a New Zealand-based marine scientist and photographer who has participated in many deep-sea expeditions. He is a co-founder of photo agency DeepSeaPhotography.com, and many of his photos appear in this book. He also is a director of DeepOcean Quest Productions.

A trained biologist, Dr. Brian Batson co-manages DeepOcean Quest Productions, a company that focuses on bringing the deep sea to life through film, animation, and educational outreach.

Photo Credits:

P4-5, © DeepSeaPhotography.com; P6-7 Twilight Zone, © DeepSeaPhotography.com; Dark Zone, © Dr. Kevin Raskoff; The Abyss, © Dr. Kevin Raskoff; P8-9 background and pressure © DeepSeaPhotography.com, Jelly, © Dr. Steven Haddock, Anglerfish and Viperfish © ImageQuestMarine.com; P10 © DeepSeaPhotography.com; P11 © Angler fish, © ImageQuestMarine.com; P12 © Dr. Steven Haddock; P13 © ImageQuestMarine.com; P14 © ImageQuestMarine.com; P15 © ImageQuestMarine.com; P16 © ImageQuestMarine.com; P17 © DeepSeaPhotography.com; P18 © DeepSeaPhotography.com; P19 © DeepSeaPhotography.com; P20 © DeepSeaPhotography.com; P21 © DeepSeaPhotography.com; P22 © DeepSeaPhotography.com; P23 © DeepSeaPhotography.com; P24 © Dr. Kevin Raskoff; P25 © Dr. Kevin Raskoff; P26 © Dr. Steven Haddock; P27 © Dr. Steven Haddock; P28 © Dr. Steven Haddock; P29 © DeepSeaPhotography.com; P30-31 © Dr. Kevin Raskoff; P32 © Dr. Steven Haddock, P33 © DeepSeaPhotography.com; P34 © DeepSeaPhotography.com; P35 © DeepSeaPhotography.com; P36 © DeepSeaPhotography.com; P37 © DeepSeaPhotography.com; P38 © DeepSeaPhotography.com; P39 © DeepSeaPhotography.com; P40 © ImageQuestMarine.com; P41 © Dr. Kevin Raskoff; P42 © DeepSeaPhotography.com; P43 © ImageQuestMarine; P44 © DeepSeaPhotography.com; P45 © Dr. Kevin Raskoff; P46 © DeepSeaPhotography.com; P47 © Dr. Steven Haddock

Dedication:

To Jacob Keane

Acknowledgment:

We'd like to thank Dr. Steven Haddock, Dr. Kevin Raskoff, and David Batson (DeepOceanQuestProductions) for their input.

THE DEEP OCEANS

North
America

Atlantic
Ocean

Pacific
Ocean

South
America

For a long time, scientists thought nothing could live in the dark, cold water. The pressure in the deep sea is like having 1,000 bowling balls on your chest. However, this strange world is home to an unbelievable collection of creatures.

This little planet we live on should be called Water, not Earth! When you look at Earth from space, our world is mostly blue. About 75 percent of our world is covered with water. Our oceans are a huge part of that.

The oceans are very deep in places. The average depth is 2½ miles (4 km). The deepest place on Earth is the Mariana Trench in the Pacific Ocean (also known as the Marianas Trench). It's more than 7 mi. (11.3 km) deep. If you dropped Mount Everest into the Mariana Trench, it would completely disappear!

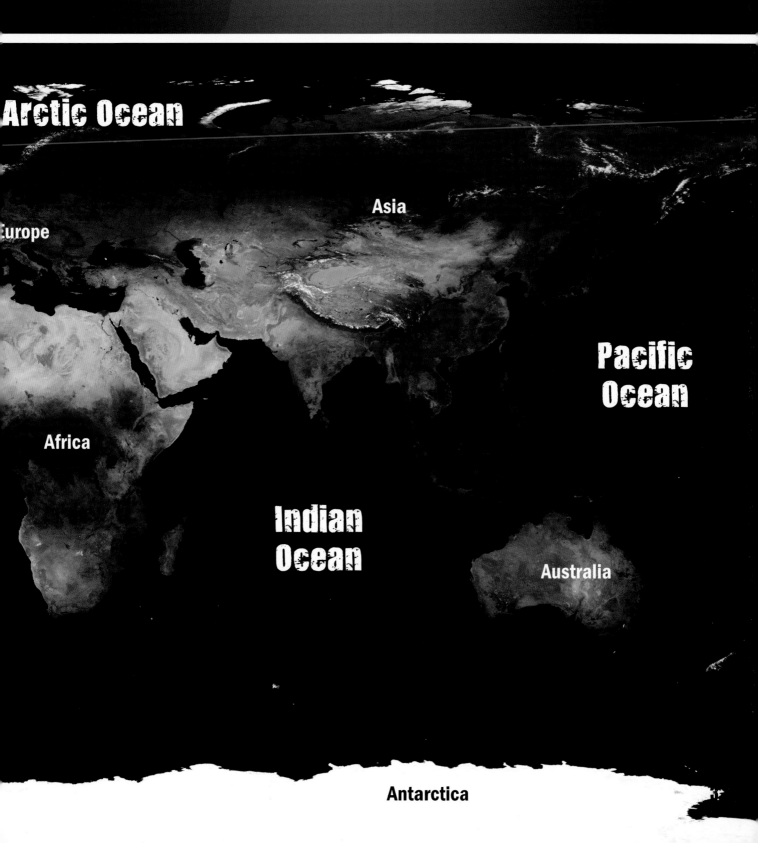

GETTING THERE

Exploring the deep sea and all of its incredible creatures takes special vehicles that can withstand the enormous pressure. Small submarines called *submersibles* and *remotely operated vehicles* (ROVs) dive down into the ocean and explore the mysteries of the deep.

The Bathyscaphe *Trieste*

The *Trieste* is a submarine that was built to go very deep. In 1960, it dove into the Mariana Trench. When it reached the bottom, its pilot saw a fishlike animal, proving that life exists under the most extreme conditions. The water pressure was more than 1,000 times greater than at the surface. That's like 350 cars sitting on you!

Submersibles, like Alvin pictured above, carry a crew of one to four people. Only five submersibles in the world can take people 2½ mi. (4 km) down to a dark, and mostly unexplored, place called the *abyss*.

ROVs are controlled from a ship at the water's surface. These robot explorers are attached to the ship on the end of a long cable. Video cameras act as the robot's eyes, showing the people on the ship what the robot is seeing and doing.

LAYERS of the OCEAN

The Twilight Zone

If you're lucky enough to dive in a submersible, you'll discover that the ocean changes as you go deeper. It gets darker and darker, and the animals get stranger and stranger....

The Twilight Zone

The Dark Zone

The Abyss

The Sunlit Zone

The upper 600 ft. (183 m) beneath the surface of the ocean is called the *sunlit zone*, or *photic* zone (photic means "light"). Tiny plants, called *phytoplankton*, live in this area. They use energy from the Sun to make food. Phytoplankton provide food for almost all other life in the ocean. It's at the bottom of the food chain.

From about 600–3,000 ft. (183–914 m) below the surface of the ocean there is still a little bit of light, but plants don't grow. Many creatures that live in this zone swim to the surface at night to feed and then return to the safety of the shadows at dawn.

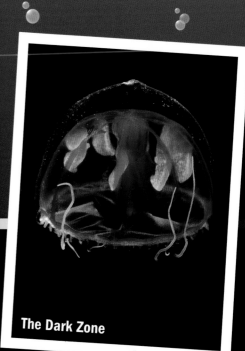

The Dark Zone

Sunlight can't reach deeper than about 3,000 ft. (914 m). Beyond that depth, it's pitch black, almost. There is light, but it comes from living creatures! Down in the dark zone at 3,000 to 13,000 ft. (914 to 3,970 km) deep, if you need light you have to make it yourself. This is called *bioluminescence* ("living light"). It appears as a blue glow.

The Abyss

The abyss is very deep, from 13,120 – 19,685 ft. (4,000 – 6,000 m). This zone never receives any light at all. There is a lot of pressure, and the temperature is a chilly 36 ˚F (2 ˚C). There is very little food to be found. Humans need special equipment to explore at this depth.

The Trench

This area is the deepest part of the world's oceans. This zone is more than 20,000 ft. (6,096 m) deep. Because of the near-freezing temperatures and crushing pressure, there are only a few creatures that can live at these depths. The creatures that make a home here wouldn't survive being brought to the low pressures at the water's surface.

What's It Like in the DEEP?

Pressure

Imagine a pile of 350 cars stacked on top of each other, with you at the bottom! That's what the water pressure is like at the bottom of the deepest parts of the ocean. You wouldn't be able to survive. But the pressure isn't a problem for the creatures that live there. They're used to it.

Pressure is a problem for deep-sea creatures only when they're brought to the surface. Many fish have gas-filled spaces in their bodies called *swim bladders* that help them float. When deep-sea creatures are brought to the surface, the change in pressure makes the gas in the swim bladder expand. The poor fish arrives with its eyes bulging and its stomach hanging out of its mouth.

Light

Sunlight is made up of many colors. Red, yellow, and green light are filtered out first. That leaves the blue light, which is why the water looks blue or blue-green. And, the deeper you go in the ocean, the less light there is. By 600 ft. (183 m), the light is very dim. At 3,000 ft. (914 m), it's pitch black.

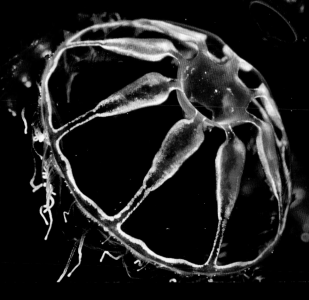

Temperature

Living in the deep sea is like living in a refrigerator! The bottom of the sea is between 36-39°F (2 to 4°C). It's the same temperature whether you're in the deep sea under the North Pole or in the deep sea around tropical islands. However, the water coming out of underwater hot springs, called *hydrothermal vents*, is about 752°F (400°C). That's hot enough to melt certain metals!

Oxygen

All animals need oxygen to breathe. In most places of the deep sea, there's plenty of oxygen. The supply of oxygen comes from deep ocean currents. The oxygenated water flows from the surface to the deep sea. If there were no currents, there wouldn't be any animals down there!

Food

The creatures of the deep ocean depend on food that drifts down from the surface zones, from tiny microscopic morsels to dead whales. The deeper you go, the less food there is. Deep-sea creatures have special tricks for surviving. When a meal arrives, it's quickly gobbled up, since it might be the last meal for a while! Many deep-sea fish have large mouths with long, pointed teeth, and a stomach that can expand to hold very large prey.

Landscape

The deep sea has high mountains, deep canyons, flat plains, active volcanoes, and hot springs. It's so dark that the lights on deep-sea submersibles and ROVs allow us to see only a little bit at a time. It's like trying to explore your neighborhood in total darkness with only a flashlight.

Most of the deep-sea floor is covered with a thick layer of mud. Hard rocks provide a solid surface to which some deep-sea creatures attach themselves. The soft mud is home to many small, burrowing animals.

HYDROTHERMAL VENTS

Hydrothermal vents are real **"hotspots"** in the cold, deep sea. Hot water gushes out of holes and cracks in the seabed at temperatures of up to 752°F (400°C). Some very unusual creatures live around these vents!

As the superheated water gushes from the vents and meets the icy cold water, it produces a dense smoke. Really hot vents produce a very black smoke. These vents are called *black smokers*. The chemicals in the water deposit around the vents and create rocky layers. These layers grow into chimneys that can be as tall as a five-story building.

A whole *ecosystem* (a group of living things that live around each other and depend on each other for food) surrounds the hydrothermal vents. The chemicals inside the Earth are a big source of energy so this ecosystem doesn't need sunlight like the *phytoplankton* at the ocean's surface.

The chemicals in the hot water are food for bacteria. The bacteria form a thick layer around the vents and float through the water in clumps, like snow.

BIOLUMINESCENCE

In the pitch black of the deep ocean, the only light comes from living creatures. This is called *bioluminescence*, or "living light."

How is bioluminescence produced?

Bioluminescence works like a glow-stick. Usually the chemicals needed to make light are made by the creature, but some use bacteria inside their bodies to do the job. This is an example of *symbiosis*, where one living thing helps out another.

In most deep-sea creatures, there are special patches called photophores. These patches are very complicated, with special lenses, mirrors, and shutters to control where and when the light is released.

Bioluminescence is common in deep-sea creatures. They're able to make their own light that they can turn on and off. They use the lights when they're in danger, or to surprise or confuse a predator.

Some deep-sea shrimp release a cloud of glowing mucus to attract the attention of a predator, allowing the shrimp to escape.

Deep-sea anglerfish use their lights to capture prey. Attached to the head is a long, thin spine that acts like a fishing rod. They have a glowing lure that acts like bait. The glowing lure attracts small fish, which are gobbled up by the large jaws full of long, pointed teeth. Other deep-sea fish use bioluminescence to find their prey, too.

Most bioluminescent creatures make blue light, but a few fish can produce red light, such as the deep-sea loose-jaw fish.

Anglerfish

Common Name: *Black devil*

Scientific Name: *Melanocetus johnsoni*

Size: 1-8 in. (3-20 cm) long

Where found: Worldwide

Depth: 1,970-9,845 ft. (600-3,000 m)

This little fish lives at extreme depths. It has a large mouth with fanglike teeth. The male of the species attaches itself to a female and lives off of her like a parasite.

Scientific Name: *Sternoptyx* sp.

Size: 2 in. (5 cm) long

Where found: Open oceans worldwide

Depth: 656–3,281 ft. (200–1,000 m)

HATCHETFISH

Some deep-sea creatures, like the hatchetfish, use bioluminescence for camouflage. The outlines of small fish that live in the twilight zone can be seen against the lighter water above. The hatchetfish can adjust the bioluminescence on its belly to match the light coming from above. It becomes almost invisible. No eating here tonight!

DEEP—SEA SQUID

This little deep sea squid has a ring of lights around each eye.

Scientific Name:
Liocranchia reinhardti

Size: 6 in. (15 cm) long

Where found: Worldwide in tropical and subtropical seas

Depth: 660 – 3,281 ft. (200 – 1,000 m)

DEEP-SEA Snaggletooth

Scientific Name:
Astronesthes niger

Size: 6 in. (15 cm) long

Where found: Atlantic Ocean

Depth: 1,640 ft. (500 m) and deeper

This small, powerful deep-sea predator has a lot of teeth and shining light organs on its body.

Endeavor coffinfish

Scientific Name: *Chaunax endeaverii*

Size: 8 - 12 in. (20 - 30 cm) long

Where found: Southwest Pacific, Australia, and Tasmania

Depth: Along the sea floor 656 - 12,926 ft. (200 - 3,940 m)

The endeavor coffinfish can inflate like a pufferfish. These fish have a small lure on their head like an anglerfish and they can walk on their front fins.

Scientific Name: *Nautilus pompilius*

Size: 8-10 in. (20-25 cm)

Where found: Indian and Pacific Oceans

Depth: Down to 1,800 ft. (550 m)

Chambered Nautilus

The chambered nautilus is a relative of the octopus and squid, but with a hard shell. It has about 90 short tentacles, which it uses to catch shrimp and fish. The chambered nautilus has remained unchanged for more than 400 million years.

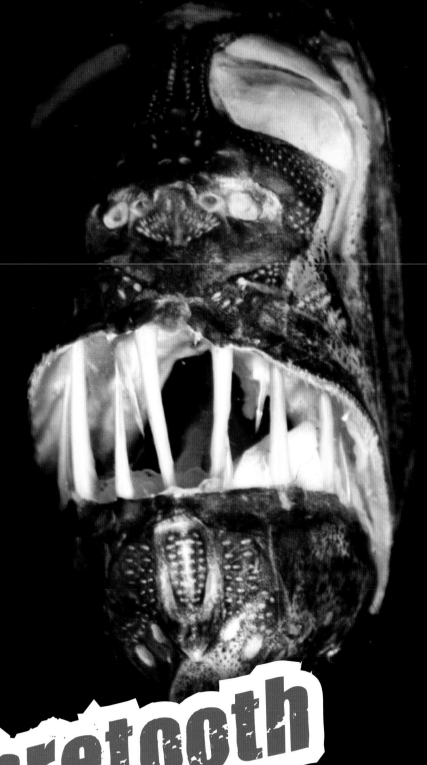

Sabretooth

Sabretooths are active twilight zone hunters. They capture and kill prey with their long fangs. The sabretooth's eyes are like a tube and face up toward the surface, possibly to see the outline of prey.

Scientific Name:
Evermannella balbo

Size: Up to 7 in. (18 cm) long

Where found: Oceans Worldwide

Depth: 660–3,280 ft. (200–1,000 m)

Orange Roughy

Scientific Name:
Hoplostethus atlanticus

Size: 25 in. (63.5 cm) long

Where found: Oceans worldwide

Depth: 656–6,562 ft. (200–2,000 m)

The orange roughy is one of the few deep-sea animals caught and eaten by humans. It grows slowly, but can live to be 150 years old. They often form large schools on undersea mountain peaks.

Vampire Squid

Scientific Name:
Vampyroteuthis infernalis

Size: Up to 12 in. (30 cm) long

Where found: Tropical and temperate oceans; photographed offshore California

Depth: 1,640–4,920 ft. (500–1,500 m)

The vampire squid is named for the thin webbing between its arms, which look like a vampire's cloak, especially when the arms and webbing are spread out to cover the head and body.

Hagfish

Scientific Name: *Eptatretus cirrhatus*

Size: Up to 40 in. (100 cm) long

Where found: Photographed off New Zealand coast

Depth: 2,625 ft. (800 m)

The hagfish feeds on the dead bodies of other animals that sink to the bottom of the ocean. It makes a huge amount of thick, gooey slime when it's upset, so it's called the snot eel. The slime protects it from predators, but it also clogs up the hagfish. From time to time, the fish has to clear the slime, so it sneezes.

Warty Anglerfish

Scientific Name: *Himantolophus groenlandicus*

Size: Up to 25 in. (60 cm) long

Where found: Tropical and temperate oceans

Depth: To 3,280 ft. (1,000 m)

The warty anglerfish has big teeth and a glowing lure to attract prey. There are many kinds of anglerfish. Some species have such big mouths that they can swallow prey bigger than they are!

DEEP-SEA Lizardfish

The deep-sea lizardfish sits on the seafloor waiting for prey to come along. When a small fish swims by, the lizardfish pounces. Its teeth are shaped like fish hooks, with a pointed triangle at the tip.

Scientific Name:
Bathysaurus mollis

Size: Up to 30 in. (75 cm) long

Where found: Temperate oceans worldwide

Depth: Usually deeper than 6,561 ft. (2,000 m)

In 2007, a gigantic squid weighing 1,000 lbs. (454 kg) was caught in Antarctica. It set a new record for the largest known *invertebrate* (an animal without a backbone).

Colossal Squid

Scientific Name: *Mesonychoteuthis hamiltoni*

Size: Up to 33 ft. (10 m) long and 2,425 lbs. (1,100 kg) in weight

Where found: Southern Ocean around Antarctica

Depth: 328–6,562 ft. (100–2,000 m)

It's not a giant squid, but the newly-named colossal squid is very heavy. This squid is a scary hunter, with sharp hooks on the ends of its tentacles for catching fish as large as a person. It's a real sea monster!

Sea Angel

Scientific Name: *Clione limacina*

Size: 2 in. (5 cm) long

Where found: Arctic, Antarctic, North Atlantic, and Eastern Pacific Oceans

Depth: 1,640 ft. (500 m)

The sea angel may look beautiful when it swims, but these swimming mollusks are fierce predators of sea butterflies.

This animal captures and kills prey with poisonous tentacles.

Colonial Jelly

Scientific Name: *Marrus sp.*

Size: 5 ft. (1.5 m) long

Where found: Arctic Ocean

Depth: 1,640 ft. (500 m)

This curious creature is actually a colony around a central stem. It's related to the jellyfish. The digestive and circulatory systems are red, but all other parts are *transparent* (see-through).

DEEP-SEA Radiolarian

Scientific Name: Unknown species

Size: $\frac{1}{2}$ in. (1.2 cm) in diameter

Where found: Waters off the coast of California

Depth: 3,281 ft. (1,000 m)

Radiolarians are not animals, but members of a group of microscopic creatures called *protozoans*. These ocean plankton have glasslike skeletons.

DEEP-SEA Octopus

Scientific Name: *Japetella heathi*
Size: 2½ in. (1.2 cm) long
Where found: Oceans worldwide
Depth: 2,297 ft. (700 m)

Like many deep-sea animals, female *Japatella* octopus can produce blue light. Scientists think this is to signal the males.

Pointy Hat Jelly

This deep-sea jellyfish has been observed from deep-diving submarines in waters deep in the Pacific Ocean.

Scientific Name: *Botrynema brucei*

Size: 1 in. (2-3 cm) in diameter

Where found: Pacific and Atlantic Oceans

Depth: 3,281-11,483 ft. (1,000-3,500 m)

Gulper Eel

Scientific Name: *Saccopharynx* sp.

Size: Up to 47 in. (120 cm) long

Where found: Deep in tropical and temperate oceans; photographed off California

Depth: Mainly between 6,560–9,842 ft. (2,000–3,000 m)

The gulper eel has a huge mouth and a stretchy stomach, so it can eat prey that's bigger than itself. This is important in the deep sea, where meals may be hard to find. Imagine eating only once every two weeks!

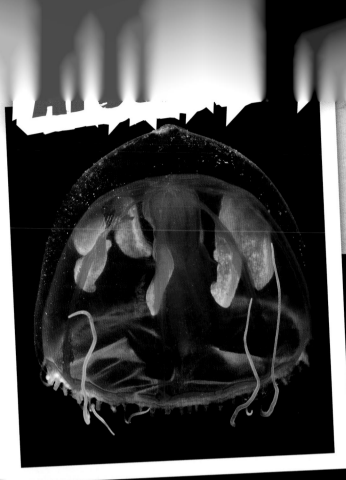

Scientific Name: *Crossota millsae*

Size: 1 in. (2.5 cm) in diameter

Where found: Arctic Ocean

Depth: 7,546 ft. (2,300 m)

Scientific Name: *Crossota norvegica*

Size: 1 in. (2.5 cm) in diameter

Where found: Arctic Ocean

Depth: 2,297 ft. (700 m)

se two jellyfish are closely related. Both live deep beneath the sea ice in the Arctic Ocean. Many p-sea animals are red in color, just like these jellies.

Scientific Name: *Aglantha* sp.

Size: $\frac{1}{2}$ in. (1.3 cm) in diameter

Where found: Arctic Ocean

Depth: Near the surface

Hydromedusa

Like all jellyfish, *Aglantha* catches animal plankton with stinging tentacles. The tentacles can be made longer for feeding or shorter for a quick getaway.

Cock-eyed Squid

The eyes of the cock-eyed squid are different sizes. The left eye is much larger than the right. Biologists think the big eye scans the surface looking for prey, while the small eye looks down. This squid is covered with hundreds of photophores.

Scientific Name:
Histioteuthis heteropsis

Size: 5 in. (12.7 cm) long

Where found: Oceans worldwide

Depth: Down to 4,100 ft. (1,250 m)

Glass Squid

Scientific Name:
Teuthowenia pellucida

Size: Up to 8 in. (20 cm) long

Where found: Waters in the southern hemisphere

Depth: 8,200 ft. (2,500 m)

The deep-sea glass squid is completely transparent.
When scared, it inflates its body into a ball and pulls its arms inside.
If it's really scared, the glass squid squirts ink. But it squirts the ink
inside its see-through body, so that it looks like a black ball floating in the darkness.

Pompeii worms can survive in water that's 176°F (80°C). This temperature is way too hot for humans.

DEEP-SEA Pompeii Worm

Scientific Name: *Alvinella pompejana*

Size: Up to 4 in. (10 cm) long

Where found: At hydrothermal vents in the Pacific Ocean

Depth: 8,200 ft. (2,500 m)

Thousands of deep-sea Pompeii worms are found around undersea hot springs or black smokers. The white hair on the worm's back is made of bacteria that feed on the chemicals in the water.

Vent Scale-Worm

Scientific Name: Polynoidae

Size: Up to $2\frac{1}{4}$ in. (6 cm) long

Where found: Near hydrothermal vents in the Pacific Ocean

Depth: 8,200 ft. (2,500 m)

This armor-plated scale-worm is found living among the giant tubeworms and mussels on hydrothermal vents. The worm's soft body is protected by tough overlapping scales. Some species of scale-worms can survive in the hot water near the tips of black smokers.

Giant Vent Worm

The giant vent worm is found on hydrothermal vents. These worms live together in large colonies. They rely on symbiotic bacteria inside their bodies for food. This animal doesn't have a mouth!

Scientific Name: *Tevnia jerichonana*

Size: Up to 91 in. (30 cm) long

Where found: Hydrothermal vents in the Pacific Ocean

Depth: 8,200 ft. (2,500 m)

Vent Eelpout

Eelpout fish are one of the few fish found at hydrothermal vents. These fish are pale and don't have scales. They feed on the invertebrates that live around the vents.

Scientific Name: *Thermarces cerberus*

Size: Up to 11 in. (30 cm) long

Where found: Hydrothermal vents in the Pacific Ocean

Depth: 8,200 ft. (2,500 m)

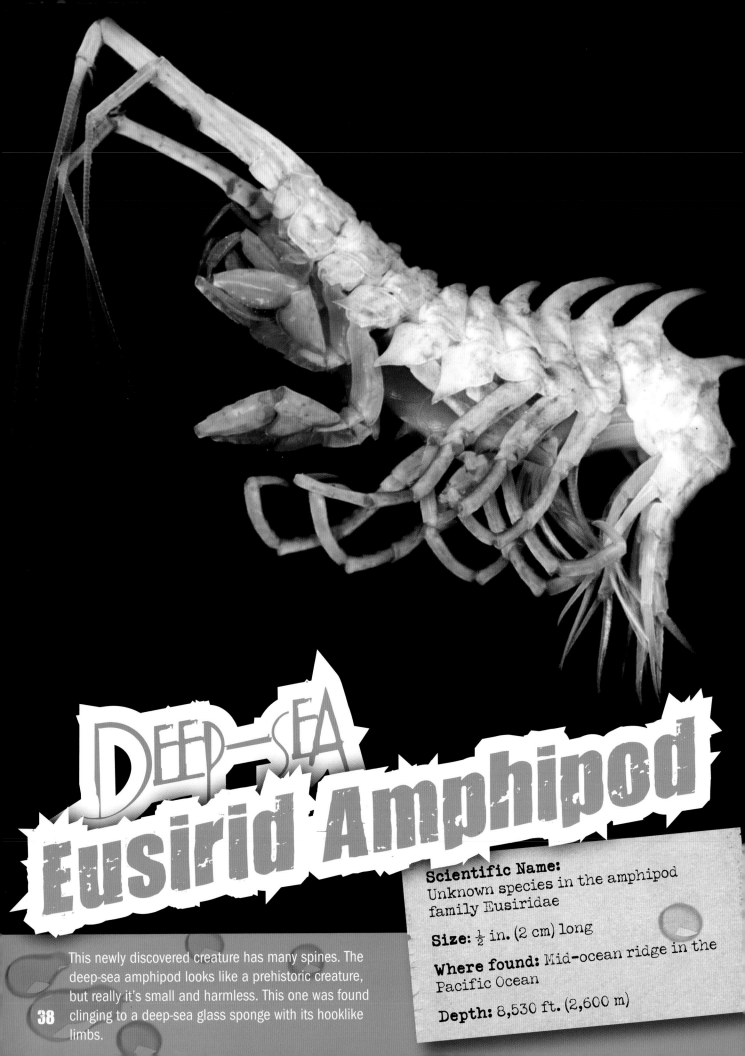

DEEP-SEA
Eusirid Amphipod

Scientific Name:
Unknown species in the amphipod family Eusiridae

Size: $\frac{1}{2}$ in. (2 cm) long

Where found: Mid-ocean ridge in the Pacific Ocean

Depth: 8,530 ft. (2,600 m)

This newly discovered creature has many spines. The deep-sea amphipod looks like a prehistoric creature, but really it's small and harmless. This one was found clinging to a deep-sea glass sponge with its hooklike limbs.

DEEP-SEA
Sea Cucumber

Deep-sea cucumbers are related to starfish and sea urchins. They eat muddy sediment and take food from it. Sea cucumbers are one of the most common creatures in the deep sea.

Scientific Name: Holothurian

Size: 2 in. (5 cm) long

Where found: Eastern tropical Pacific Ocean

Depth: 8,530 ft. (2,600 m)

Viperfish

This ferocious predator has fangs that are so large, they can't fit inside its mouth. The viperfish has a long fishing lure tipped with a photophore. During the day, the viperfish is found deep in the ocean, but it travels up at night, where there is more food.

Scientific Name: *Chauliodus sloani*

Size: 12-24 in. (30-60 cm) long

Where found: Worldwide

Depth: 250 – 5,000 ft. (76 – 1,500 m)

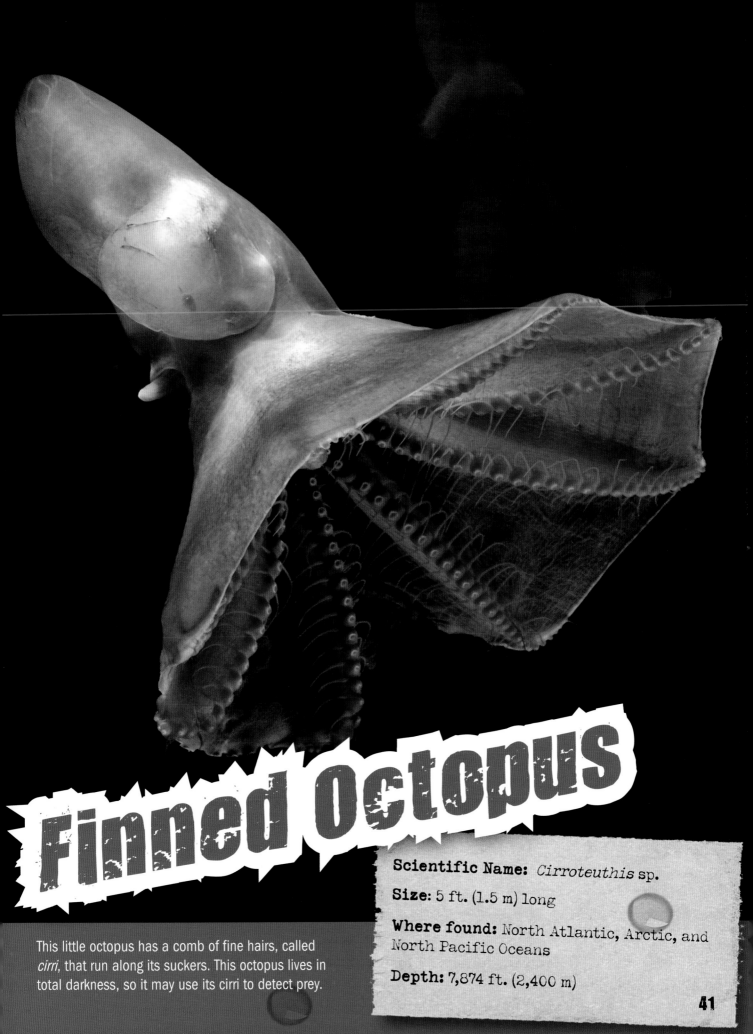

Finned Octopus

This little octopus has a comb of fine hairs, called *cirri*, that run along its suckers. This octopus lives in total darkness, so it may use its cirri to detect prey.

Scientific Name: *Cirroteuthis* sp.

Size: 5 ft. (1.5 m) long

Where found: North Atlantic, Arctic, and North Pacific Oceans

Depth: 7,874 ft. (2,400 m)

Comb Jelly

The beautiful comb jelly is actually a fierce predator. Unlike true jellyfish, it does not have stinging tentacles, but it does have a very large mouth to gobble up other jellies. When it's upset, the comb jelly puts on a beautiful light show of bioluminescence.

Scientific Name: *Beroe* sp.

Size: Up to 4 in. (10 cm) long

Where found: North Atlantic, Arctic, and North Pacific Oceans

Depth: Down to 820 ft. (250 m)

PACIFIC Seadragon

The Pacific seadragon feeds on small fish, shrimp, and krill. It has a glowing lure under its chin that helps attract prey. The male Pacific seadragon are much smaller than the females and don't have any teeth.

Scientific Name: *Idiacanthus antostromus*

Size: 14 in. (35.5 cm) long

Where found: Pacific Ocean

Depth: 1,640 ft. (500 m)

Dumbo Octopus

The Dumbo octopus is the deepest known. It's named after Disney's famous cartoon elephant because of the giant ears. The Dumbo octopus glides through the deep sea by flapping its earlike fins. It goes down to the seafloor to feed.

Scientific Name: *Grimpoteuthis* sp.

Size: Up to 9 in. (25 cm) across

Where found: Oceans worldwide; photographed in the Eastern Pacific Ocean

Depth: 16,400 ft. (5,000 m)

Unknown Species

This is a newly discovered deep-sea comb jelly. It is so new that not much is known about it. Scientists do know that it swims by beating its eight combs, which are made of rows of short paddles.

Scientific Name: Cydippid

Size: 1 in. (2.5 cm) in diameter

Where found: Discovered in Arctic Ocean

Depth: 5,905 ft. (1,800 m)

DEEP-SEA ISOPOD

Scientific Name: *Acutiserolis bromleyana*

Size: Up 2 in. (6 cm) long

Where found: Muddy sediment in the deep sea

Depth: 3,280 ft. (1,000 m)

These strange animals live on the deep seafloor. They look like trilobites, which became extinct millions of years ago. These isopods are closely related to common pill bugs and woodlice found on land under rotting logs.

Shelled Sea Butterfly

The sea butterfly is a kind of swimming snail. It has a very thin shell and two muscular fins to swim through the water. To feed, it makes a net out of mucus to catch plankton.

Scientific Name: *Cavolinia* sp.
Size: $\frac{1}{2}$ in. (1.5 cm) in diameter
Where found: Oceans worldwide
Depth: 328 ft. (100 m)

GLOSSARY

Bioluminescence: The blue, green, or red light made by a living creature.

Biomass: The total weight of living matter present in one area.

Black smoker: A hot hydrothermal vent that releases fine black particles that look like smoke. Black smokers often look like chimneys.

Camouflage: The ability of a creature to disguise itself by blending into the background.

Hydrothermal vent: Where hot water and dissolved minerals pour out of holes in the seafloor. The vents often are surrounded by animals that get their energy from the minerals.

Mesopelagic zone: The twilight zone of the ocean, where light is too dim for plants to grow but bright enough to be visible to many deep-sea creatures. It's normally found between 656 and 3,280 ft. (200 and 1,000 m) deep.

Microscopic: Too small to be seen without a microscope.

Mollusk: A soft-bodied unsegmented invertebrate (animal without a backbone), often with a shell. Familiar examples are clams, mussels, slugs, and snails, but octopuses and squids are also mollusks.

Oxygen: The gas breathed by animals (including humans) to stay alive. In the sea, it's dissolved in seawater.

Photic zone: The top 656 ft. (200 m) of the ocean, where there is enough sunlight for phytoplankton to grow.

Photophores: Light-producing organs on the bodies of many kinds of deep-sea fish, squids, and octopuses.

Phytoplankton: Microscopic plants that make their food using the energy from sunlight.

Predator: An animal that eats other animals.

Prey: An animal that is eaten by other animals.

Remotely operated vehicles (ROVs): Undersea robots used to explore deep or dangerous parts of the ocean. They don't carry people and are usually attached by cables to a surface ship.

Submersibles: Small, battery-powered submarines that can take a group of people into the deep sea.

Symbiosis: When animals of two different species live together. Often one or both of the animals benefit from the arrangement.